TO THIS DAY

FOR THE BULLIED AND BEAUTIFUL

SHANE KOYCZAN

WALKER BOOKS
AND SUBSIDIARIES

LONDON • BOSTON • SYDNEY • AUCKLAND

First published in Great Britain 2014 by Walker Books Ltd
87 Vauxhall Walk, London SE11 5HJ

10 9 8 7 6 5 4 3 2 1

Originally published in North America by: Annick Press Ltd.
© 2014 Shane Koyczan (text) and multiple illustrators (art)/
Annick Press Ltd.

Printed in China

British Library Cataloguing in Publication Data:
a catalogue record for this book is available
from the British Library

ISBN 978-1-4063-5812-4

www.walker.co.uk

GREETINGS

My name is Shane Koyczan. I'm a spoken-word poet, which means I write poems and perform them on stage for audiences all over the world. The poem in this book, "To This Day", is about my experience of being bullied as a kid.

I can't remember how old I was when I started writing. I know that I was very young. My grandparents raised me and writing became something that my grandmother always encouraged. Writing was a way to escape my real life, a way to cope with cruelty and indifference. Sometimes even worse than the people who hurt you are the people who don't care that you're being hurt – the ones who *could* do something but choose not to. I understand it; sometimes you don't want to get involved and risk having bullies shift their attention to you. That's normal ... that's fear. I was afraid a lot when I was growing up.

OVER HALF OF STUDENTS HAVE WITNESSED BULLYING AT SCHOOL

I didn't have many friends when I was in school, and I was often picked on and made fun of. I had to learn how to be my own friend. The way I did that was through writing. I could create my own world, and make myself the hero of the story. What I wrote as a kid was mostly just fragments — short sentences about the way I felt. As I got older I started to put those thoughts and ideas into poems. Today I am amazed to see how many people in the world feel the same way I do. I'm astonished by how connected we are through the things we've endured.

I wrote "To This Day" to show people the kind of connection I'd experienced throughout my travels as a poet and performer. At every performance I was met by others who wanted to share their stories about what they'd been through. And while our experiences may not have been identical, I came to realize that they were a way to help us understand one another.

Eventually I brought the poem to my band (Shane Koyczan and The Short Story Long) and they built music around it. The resulting piece was released on the album *Remembrance Year*. Soon after, I started to receive mail about it. The response from strangers was beautiful and made me want to share the poem on a broader scale. So the idea came to crowdsource short animations that could be woven together to create one fluid video. Eighty-six animators and motion artists from around the world donated their time and considerable talent to create something that would speak to those who felt they were alone. Over 12 million hits later it's

85 PERCENT OF BULLYING HAPPENS WHILE OTHER KIDS ARE WATCHING

*Bullying facts from **bullying.org** and **bullyingstatistics.org***

continuing to speak. My gratitude to all the artists involved is endless. Thank you for creating something that has helped so many. This work will stand as a testament of what a community of caring people can achieve.

1 IN 7 KIDS HAS EITHER BEEN A VICTIM OF BULLYING OR A BULLY

This book is a continuation of that collaborative project. The thirty artists whose work appears here come from all over the world. Each was assigned a section of the poem to illustrate in his or her own style. All of them brought a wonderfully unique and heartfelt interpretation to my words. Several artists also contributed anecdotes about their own experiences with bullying. You'll find their quotes at the end of the book.

I didn't realize it at the time, but writing became the way I could stand up for myself. Self-expression showed me a world that values what I think, and feels what I feel — it makes the world my friend. I realize that you might not be a writer, but in some way you are an artist. The trick is to find your medium, to figure out what helps you express yourself, whether it's art, music, dance, photography, or some other creative form. In order to find your voice you first have to explore. Look everywhere. Realize that not all languages contain words, and that other people may have trouble translating what you've said. Be patient. Fear will tempt you into silence.

BULLYING WILL USUALLY STOP WITHIN 10 SECONDS IF SOMEONE STEPS IN TO HELP THE VICTIM

Remember that the world will never hear you if you choose to say nothing.

WHEN I WAS A KID
I USED TO THINK THAT PORK CHOPS AND KARATE CHOPS
WERE THE SAME THING
I THOUGHT THEY WERE BOTH PORK CHOPS
AND BECAUSE MY GRANDMOTHER THOUGHT IT WAS CUTE
AND BECAUSE THEY WERE MY FAVORITE
SHE LET ME KEEP DOING IT
NOT REALLY A **BIG DEAL**

One day

before I realized fat kids are not

designed to climb trees

I fell out of a tree

and bruised the right side of my body

I didn't want to tell my grandmother about it

because I was afraid I'd get in trouble

for playing somewhere that I shouldn't have been

a few days later

the gym teacher

noticed the bruise

and I got sent to

the principal's office

FROM THERE I WAS SENT TO ANOTHER SMALL ROOM
WITH A REALLY NICE LADY
WHO ASKED ME ALL KINDS OF QUESTIONS
ABOUT MY LIFE AT HOME

I SAW NO
REASON
TO LIE

9

As far as I was concerned
life was pretty good
I told her "whenever I'm sad
my grandmother gives me karate chops"
this led to a full scale investigation
and I was removed from the house
for three days
until they finally decided to ask
how I got the bruises

news of this silly little story

quickly spread through the school

and I earned my first nickname

"PORK CHOP"!

to this day

I ~~HATE~~ PORK CHOPS

I'm not the only kid
who grew up this way

surrounded by people who used to say
that rhyme about sticks

and stones

as it broken bones

hurt more than the

names we got called

and we got called them all

15

so we grew up believing no one
would ever fall in love with us
that we'd be lonely forever
that we'd never meet someone
to make us feel like the sun
was something they built for us
in their tool shed

SO BROKEN HEART STRINGS BLED THE BLUES
AS WE TRIED TO EMPTY OURSELVES
SO WE WOULD FEEL NOTHING
DON'T TELL ME THAT HURTS LESS THAN A BROKEN BONE
THAT AN INGROWN LIFE
IS SOMETHING SURGEONS CAN CUT AWAY
THAT THERE'S NO WAY FOR IT TO METASTASIZE

IT DOES.

she was eight
years old
our first day of
grade three when
she got called ugly

We both got moved to the back of the class
so we would stop getting bombarded by spit balls

but the school halls were a battleground
where we found ourselves outnumbered
day after wretched day

WE USED TO STAY INSIDE FOR RECESS
BECAUSE OUTSIDE WAS WORSE
OUTSIDE WE'D HAVE TO REHEARSE

RUNNING
AWAY

OR LEARN TO STAY STILL LIKE STATUES

GIVING NO CLUES THAT WE WERE THERE

In grade five they taped

a sign to her desk that read

BEWARE OF dog

because of a birthmark
that takes up a little less than half
of her face
kids used to say she looks like a

wrong
answer

that someone tried to erase
but couldn't quite get the job done

AND they'll
never UNDERSTAND
That she's RAISING
two kids
WHOSE definition
of BEAUTY
Begins WITH the
word MOM
Because they SEE
her HEART
Before THEY see
her SKIN
That SHE'S only
ever always
been AMAZING

HE WAS A BROKEN BRANCH

GRAFTED ONTO A DIFFERENT FAMILY TREE

ADOPTED
BUT NOT BECAUSE HIS PARENTS OPTED FOR
A DIFFERENT DESTINY
HE WAS THREE WHEN HE BECAME A MIXED DRINK
OF ONE PART LEFT ALONE

AND TWO PARTS TRAGEDY

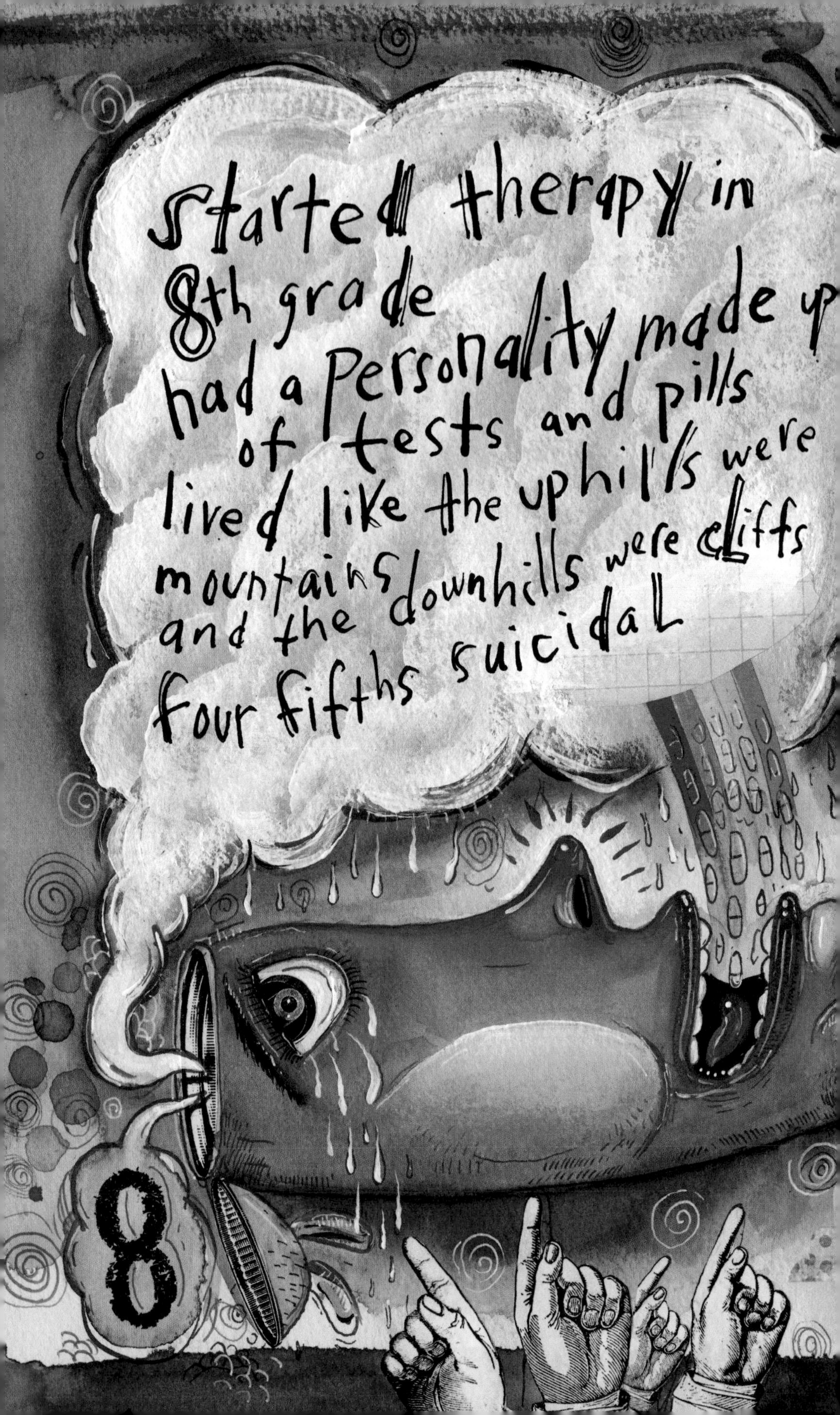
started therapy in
8th grade
had a personality made up
of tests and pills
lived like the uphills were
mountains downhills were cliffs
and the
four fifths suicidal
8

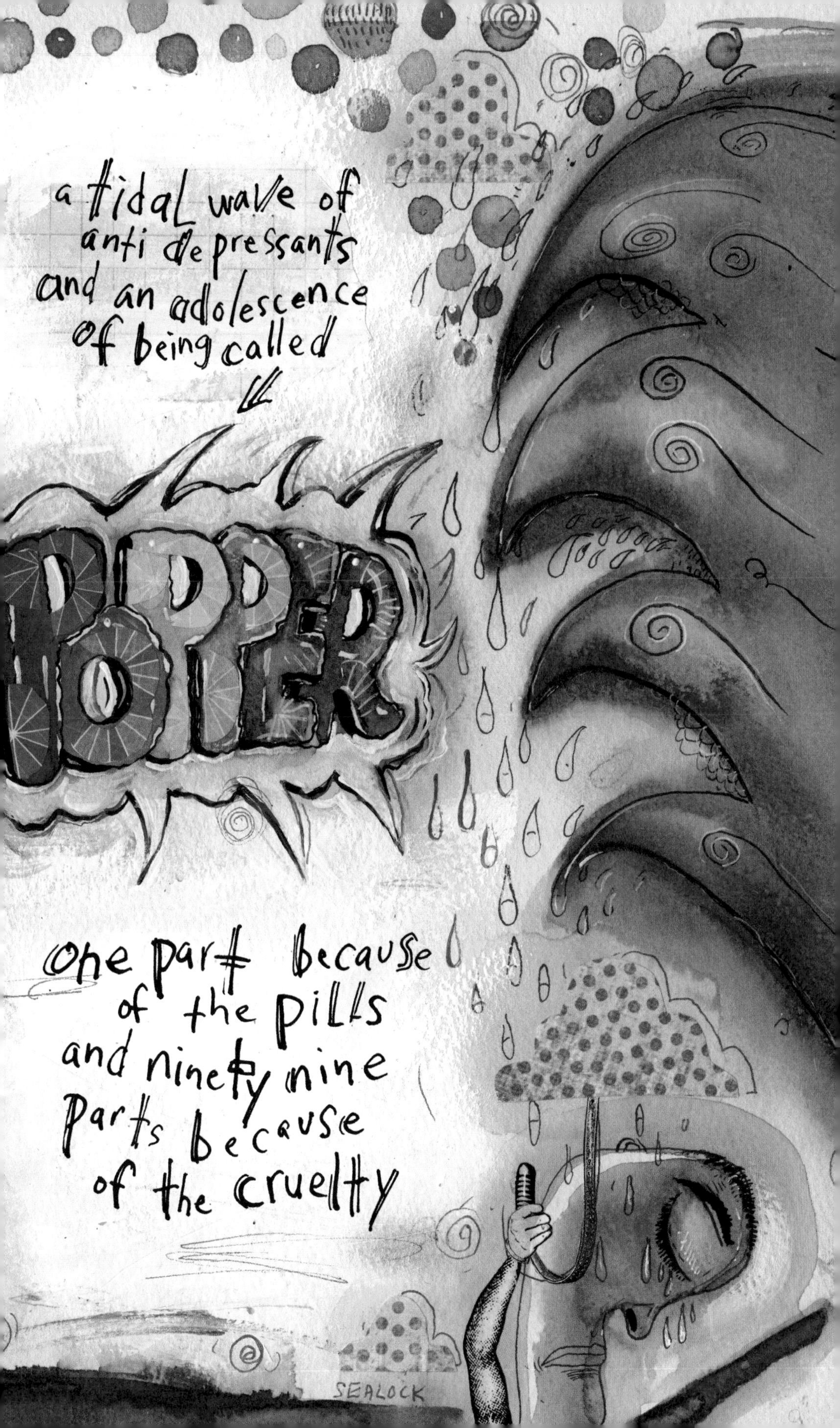

a tidal wave of anti depressants and an adolescence of being called

POPPER

one part because of the pills and ninety nine parts because of the cruelty

SEALOCK

he tried to kill himself in grade ten
when a kid who still had
his mom and dad
had the audacity to
tell him "get over it"

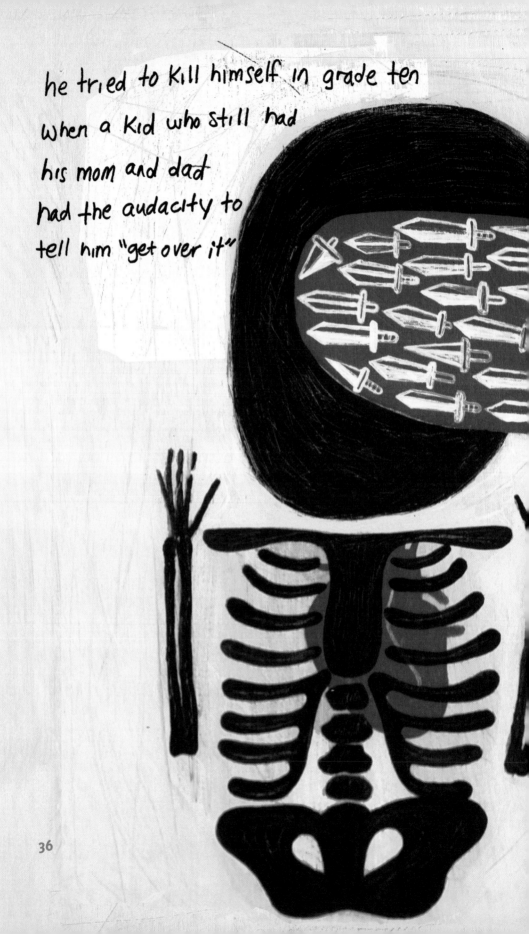

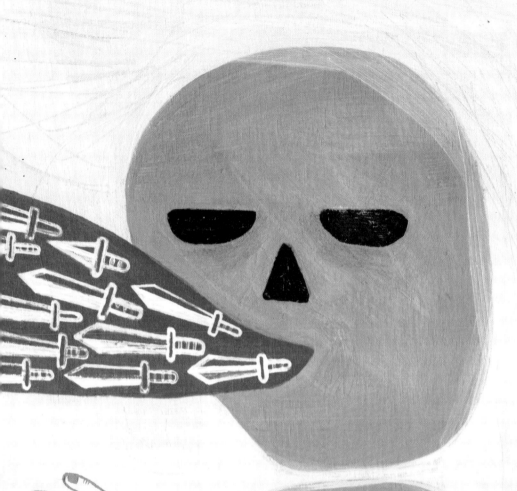

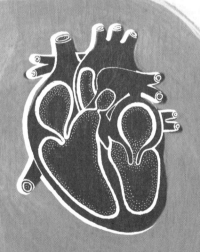

as if depression
is something that
can be remedied
by any of the
contents found in
a first aid kit

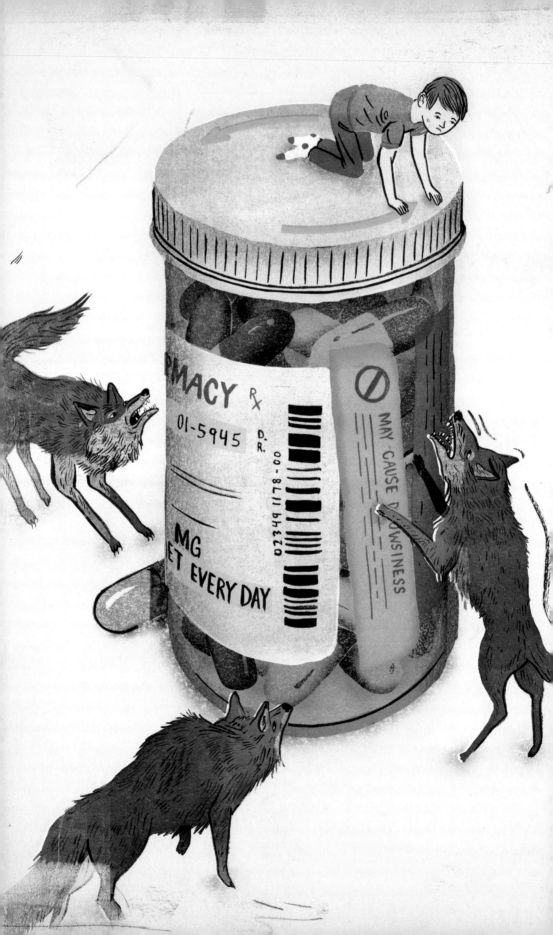

and despite an army of friends
who all call him an inspiration
he remains a conversation piece between people
who can't understand

sometimes becoming drug free
has less to do with addiction
and more to do with

sanity

We weren't
the _only_ kids
who grew up
this way.

to this day

kids are still being called names

the classics were

hey stupid

hey spaz

seems like each school
  has an arsenal of names
 getting updated every year
and if a kid breaks in a school
and no one around <u>chooses</u> to hear.
   do they make a sound ?
  are they just the background noise
of a soundtrack stuck on repeat
 when people say things like

  kids can be cruel ?

EVERY SCHOOL WAS A BIG TOP
CIRCUS TENT
AND THE PECKING ORDER WENT

FROM ACROBATS

TO LION TAMERS

FROM CLOWNS

TO CARNIES

ALL OF THESE WERE MILES
AHEAD OF WHO WE WERE

We were freaks
lobster claw boys
and bearded ladies

Oddities

juggling depression and loneliness
playing solitaire spin the bottle
trying to kiss the
wounded parts
of ourselves and heal

but at night
while the others slept

we kept walking the tightrope

it was practice

and yeah
some of us

fell

But I want to tell them
that all of this
is just debris
leftover when we finally
    decide to smash
all the things we thought
we used to be
and if you can't see anything
    beautiful about yourself
get a better mirror
look a little closer

    stare a   little longer

because there's something inside you

that made you keep trying

despite everyone who told you to quit

you built a cast around your

broken heart

and signed it yourself

you signed it

"THEY WERE WRONG"

BECAUSE MAYBE YOU DIDN'T BELONG TO A GROUP OR A CLIQUE

MAYBE THEY DECIDED TO PICK YOU LAST FOR BASKETBALL

OR FOR EVERYTHING

MAYBE YOU USED TO BRING BRUISES AND BROKEN TEETH

TO SHOW AND TELL BUT NEVER TOLD

BECAUSE HOW CAN YOU HOLD YOUR GROUND

IF EVERYONE AROUND YOU WANTS TO BURY YOU BENEATH IT

YOU HAVE TO BELIEVE THAT THEY WERE WRONG

THEY HAVE TO BE WRONG

WHY ELSE WOULD WE STILL BE HERE?

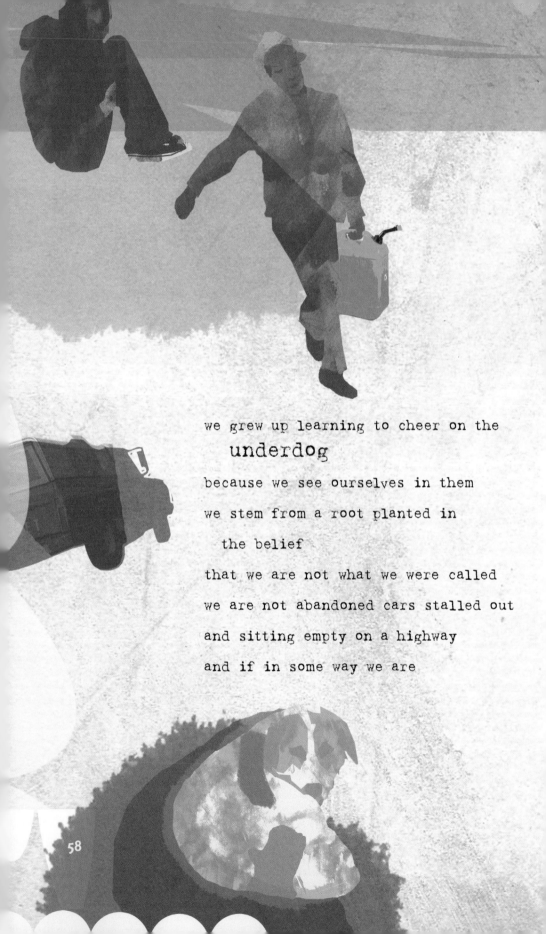

we grew up learning to cheer on the
underdog

because we see ourselves in them

we stem from a root planted in

the belief

that we are not what we were called

we are not abandoned cars stalled out

and sitting empty on a highway

and if in some way we are

don't worry

we only got out to walk   and get gas

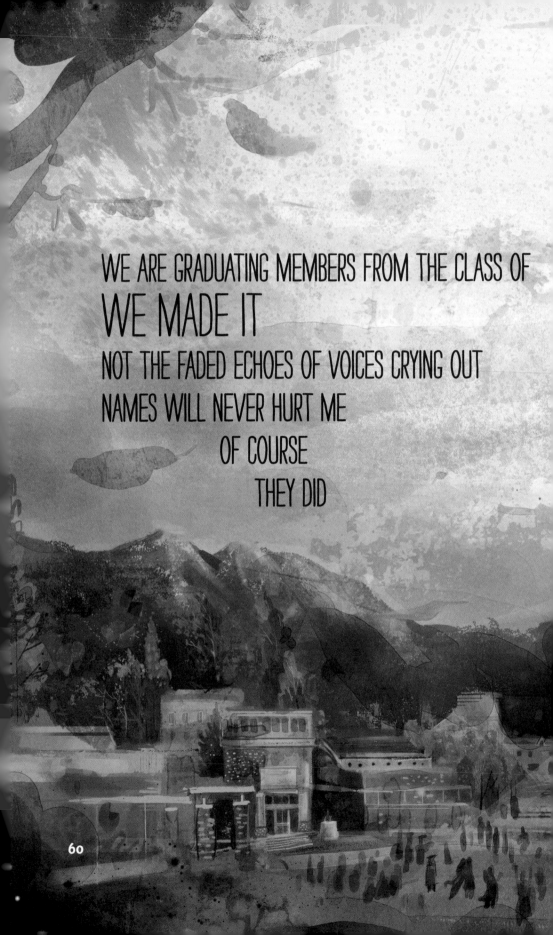

WE ARE GRADUATING MEMBERS FROM THE CLASS OF
WE MADE IT
NOT THE FADED ECHOES OF VOICES CRYING OUT
NAMES WILL NEVER HURT ME
OF COURSE
THEY DID

BUT OUR LIVES WILL ONLY EVER
ALWAYS
CONTINUE TO BE
A BALANCING ACT
THAT HAS LESS TO DO WITH PAIN
AND MORE TO DO WITH

Beauty

THE STORY OF TO THIS DAY

To This Day began life as a spoken-word poem on Shane Koyczan's 2009 album *Shut Up And Say Something*. It was later rerecorded with music for the 2012 album *Remembrance Year* and published that same year in the poetry collection *Our Deathbeds Will Be Thirsty*. Soon after, it was turned into a video, with Shane's reading of the poem complemented by visuals created by dozens of animators from around the world. The video went live on YouTube on February 19, 2013, to mark Pink Shirt Day, an initiative started by two Canadian students to raise awareness about bullying. The original intent of the poem had been simply, in Shane's words, to "put an arm around the shoulder of somebody who needs it." But what happened next could not have been predicted by anyone.

Almost immediately, the video went viral. Within two days, it received 1.4 million hits. Shane's message about bullying and its long-lasting effects quickly spread across the Internet and beyond; the video was featured on nearly every major website, shared through social media, and even covered on television news programs. By the end of March, the video had been viewed over 7 million times, and the numbers kept growing.

We asked the illustrators for *To This Day* to share their own personal stories about bullying. →

When I was in grade seven, one of the girls in my class taped a note to the front of my desk that read, "Cindy has a big bum." I remember first feeling shocked that someone would take the time to be so cruel, and then feeling gutted. Up to that point, I had felt pretty good about my bum. The same girl accused me, in front of an audience, of wearing bargain basement shoes. The secret was out: I wasn't one of *them*.

– Cinders McLeod

The response to the video was not only overwhelming; it was also intensely personal. Hundreds of people were moved to write to Shane and thank him for writing the poem. Tens of thousands more left comments online or sent messages or tweets. Many kids, teens, parents and teachers wrote of the profound way in which Shane's words captured their own experiences of bullying. "To This Day" became a rallying cry for the rapidly growing movement against bullying in schools.

In February of 2013, just after the video went viral, Shane performed at the TED2013 Conference in California. The influential TED organization (best known for its TED Talks, short presentations by innovative speakers and performers) had invited Shane to its annual gathering of young thinkers and artists from around the world. In his presentation, Shane explained how he came to write "To This Day", and performed the poem live with musical accompaniment. His emotional performance brought the audience to their feet, and many to tears. The online video of his talk was later viewed over 1.3 million times.

The project received wide acclaim both for its artistic excellence and for its positive social message. The video won a Webcuts.13 Award — presented every year to the six best Internet movies from around the world — for Best Collaborative Project. And in 2013, Shane was awarded the British Columbia Civil Liberties Association's Liberty

Award for the Arts, which recognizes outstanding leadership to promote human rights and freedoms, on the strength of "To This Day" and its message against bullying.

No doubt the enormous resonance of "To This Day" stems from the sad prevalence of bullying in our society. Nearly everyone experiences bullying at some point in their lives, whether it's as a victim, a perpetrator, or a bystander. Bullying comes in many different forms, from name-calling to social shunning, from threats to physical violence. It happens in schools, in homes, in workplaces, and in every corner of the Internet.

In the past, bullying incidents among kids and teens were often written off by adults. Insults and even physical violence were seen as "a normal part of growing up" or "a rite of passage," and kids were expected to endure them without complaint. But over the past few years there has been a growing awareness of the problem of bullying and its deeply harmful effects. Bullying victims have been shown to be at a higher risk for depression, self-harming and suicide. Some victims may turn to bullying or other forms of violence themselves, creating never-ending cycles of revenge. And these issues can continue into adulthood — statistics show that three in five childhood bullies have had at least one criminal conviction by their mid-twenties. It's no surprise that numerous groups have taken an interest in preventing bullying where it starts.

Many schools, cities, provinces and states now participate in events like Pink Shirt Day or Bullying Awareness Week, and actively promote the idea that kids have the right to learn in safe environments.

"I was often one of the last picked for any team sport. By the time they got to me there was an unenthusiastic "I guess we'll take so-and-so." It really sucks to have that "I guess" before your name, no matter how old you are."
— Kyle Metcalf

"When I was a child, a boy sometimes got on our school bus. He was very small and his clothes were dirty. No one wanted him to sit next to them. I knew it was cowardly not to stick up for him; he had to sit somewhere. I can't even say who started this bullying, but it grew until almost everyone took part. Later I was glad to hear that this boy had grown up into a very attractive man. To this day, I feel ashamed of what happened on that bus. "
— Anonymous

I remember being part of a group of kids and shouting out rhymes on the school steps to make another kid feel bad. I don't know why we taunted him – he might have once picked his nose, and the rhyme was about that. I never took into account that it was hurtful. "
— Katy Dockrill

Various organizations, helplines and websites now exist to raise awareness and understanding of the issue.

But schools and families are in desperate need of tools to confront the problem. *To This Day* is a starting point, a way to begin the conversation. Through this book, and the ever-growing network of young people, educators and advocates, we can send a message that will have a far-reaching and long-lasting impact.

There *is* something kids can do about bullying. By standing up for themselves and others, by supporting each other, and by saying out loud that bullying is *not* a normal part of life, that no one should have to put up with it, kids can make a difference.

In grade school I was a target for some of the meaner kids. Then in high school, I moved away from the people who were making my life hell. I decided not to care what people thought of me, and to focus on all the great things I wanted to become. "
— Drew Shannon

"When I was about ten, three slightly younger boys would gang up and try to push me around. I don't think it occurred to me to tell anyone. It seemed like my own problem that I somehow had to get through."
— Gary Venn

RESOURCES

Alex Holmes' campaign: Having been bullied himself, teenager Alex Holmes decided to take a stand. He invented a role at his school called "Student Anti-Bullying Coordinator". Then he started organizing events, creating videos, running campaigns and getting other students involved as ambassadors, event leaders and bully "patrollers". This changed not only his life, but the lives of many others at his school, in his country, and around the world. **www.inspiremykids. com/2010/alex-holmes-making-a-stand-from-bullied-to-anti-bullying-leader/**

BeatBullying: BeatBullying is an international bullying prevention charity working and campaigning to make bullying unacceptable, in the UK and across Europe. On the BeatBullying website you can speak to a cybermentor. Cybermentors are young people you can chat to if you're being cyberbullied or bullied in any other way. They will help you work out what to do next. **www.beatbullying.org**

Bullybusters: Bullybusters operates a free anti-bullying helpline for anyone who's been affected by bullying. It also has a website and message board, with sections specifically for children and young people. **0800 1696928**

BullyingUK: Part of the family lives website, BullyingUK offers information and advice on all forms of bullying including cyberbullying **www.bullying.co.uk**

Child Exploitation and Online Protection (CEOP) Centre's ThinkUKnow website: CEOP works with child protection partners across the UK and overseas to identify the main threats to children and coordinates activity against these threats to bring offenders to account. They protect children from harm online and offline, directly through National Crime Agency led operations and in partnership with local and international agencies. **www.thinkuknow.co.uk**

ChildLine: ChildLine is a private and confidential service for children and young people up to the age of nineteen. You can contact a ChildLine counsellor about anything – no problem is too big or too small. **www.childline.org.uk** or call their free helpline **0800 1111**

Kidscape: Kidscape was the first charity in the UK established specifically to prevent bullying and child sexual abuse. Kidscape's website has lots of advice on bullying for children and young people, including tips on what to do if you're bullied, on moving schools and making friends. **www.kidscape.org.uk**

National Health Service: The NHS website is a great place to find clear and helpful information about bullying and advice on how to stop it. **www.nhs.uk/livewell/bullying**

ILLUSTRATOR CREDITS

4–5 © Andrea Wan, Germany, andreawan.com

6–7 © Drew Shannon, Canada, drewshannon.ca

8–9 © Gary Venn, New Zealand, garyvennillustration.com

10–11 © Gillian Newland, Canada, gilliannewland.com

12–13 © Greg Stevenson, Canada, gregstevenson.com

14–15 © Kim Rosen, USA, kimrosen.com

16–17 © Satoshi Kitamura, Japan

18–19 © Barroux, France, barroux.info

20–21 © Glenda Tse, Canada, glendatse.com

22–23 © Scott Waters, Canada, scottwaters.ca

24–25 © Armin Greder, Peru

26–27 © Cinders McLeod, Canada, cindersmcleod.com

28–29 © Gemma Correll, United Kingdom, gemmacorrell.com

30–31 © Katy Dockrill, Canada, katydockrill.com

32–33 © Eric Diotte, Canada, ericdiotte.com

34–35 © Rick Sealock, Canada, ricksealock.com

36–37 © Sara Guindon, USA, saraguindon.com

38–39 © Mike Freiheit, USA, mikefreiheit.com

40–41 © Byron Eggenschwiler, Canada, byronegg.com

42–43 © Monika Melnychuk, Canada, monikamelnychuk.com

44–45 © Kathleen Jennings, Australia, tanaudel.wordpress.com

46–47 © Sarah Leavitt, Canada, sarahleavitt.com

48–49 © Meghan Lands, Canada, meghanlands.com

50–51 © Carol Adlam, United Kingdom, caroladlam.co.uk

52–53 © Phil Lesnie, Australia, phillesnie.tumblr.com

54–55 © Kim Stewart, Canada, kimstewartonline.ca

56–57 © Kyle Metcalf, Canada, kylemetcalf.com

58–59 © Karen Hibbard, Canada, karenhibbard.com

60–61 © Dongjun Lee, Canada, illudj.com

62–63 © Taryn Gee, Canada, taryngee.com

For more information, visit **www.walker.co.uk/authorsartists**

ABOUT THE AUTHOR

Shane Koyczan is an award-winning poet, author and spoken-word performer. He was born in Yellowknife, Northwest Territories, in 1976, and began writing as a child.

Shane's performances have brought audiences to their feet in New York, London, Edinburgh, Sydney and Los Angeles, to name just a few places. He received five-star reviews for his performance at the Edinburgh Fringe Festival, and he is the winner of both the U.S. National Poetry Slam and the Canadian Spoken Word Olympics. At the opening ceremonies of the 2010 Winter Olympics in Vancouver, British Columbia, Shane wowed a worldwide audience of more than 1 billion with his performance of his poem "We Are More".

Shane is also the author of several books, including a novel in verse, *Stickboy*, about a bullied kid who becomes a bully. *Stickboy* has been hailed by teachers, academics and mental health experts for its deft handling of the subject of bullying. In 2013, Shane's work was selected for inclusion in Amnesty International's Artists for Amnesty campaign, which supports freedom of expression around the world.

Today, Shane travels the globe performing his poetry, sometimes alone and sometimes with his band Shane Koyczan and the Short Story Long. He lives in Penticton, British Columbia.

LINKS

Shane's website: **shanekoyczan.com**

"To This Day" video: **tothisdayproject.com/the_video.html**

iPhone app for "To This Day": **tothisdayproject.com**

Shane's TED Talk: **ted.com/talks/shane_koyczan_to_this_day_for_ the_bullied_and_beautiful.html**

TED Ed lesson on "To This Day": **ed.ted.com/featured/po4GkFoj**

Follow Shane on Twitter: **twitter.com/Koyczan**

The audio version of the poem is available on the album *Remembrance Year*: **http://shanekoyczan.shop.redstarmerch.com.** Or download the track from iTunes.